My First...
Visit to the Hospital

Published in the United States by
QEB Publishing, Inc.
3 Wrigley, Suite A
Irvine, CA 92618

www.qeb-publishing.com

Library of Congress Cataloging-in-Publication Data

Marleau, Eve.
  Visit to the hospital / by Eve Marleau ; illustrated by Michael
Garton.
    p. cm. -- (QEB my first-)
  Summary: When Aisha hurts her arm in an accidental fall,
her mother takes her to the hospital to check if is is broken.
  ISBN 978-1-59566-986-5 (hardcover)
  [1. Accidents--Fiction. 2. Medical care--Fiction.] I. Garton,
Michael, ill. II. Title.
  PZ7.M34435Vm 2010
  [E]--dc22

                        2008056081

Author Eve Marleau
Illustrator Michael Garton
Consultants Shirley Bickler, Joanne Brougham
                  and Tracey Dils
Designer Elaine Wilkinson

Publisher Steve Evans
Creative Director Zeta Davies
Managing Editor Amanda Askew

Printed and bound in China

The words in **bold** are
explained in the glossary
on page 24.

My First...

Visit to the Hospital

Eve Marleau and Michael Garton

QEB Publishing

Aisha and her brother Amir love to play catch with their green Frisbee.

"Hey! Over here, Amir!"

Sometimes, Amir throws the Frisbee...

really high,

or really wide,

or very, very fast!

5

Amir throws the Frisbee
much too high. Aisha walks
backward, her foot slips, and…

wallop!

She falls over the yard chair.

6

"Ow, ow!"

"My arm hurts!"
Aisha starts to cry.

7

"Mom, it hurts so much!"

"Oh dear, Aisha. Your arm could be broken. Let's go to the hospital to have it checked."

Aisha looks worried.

"It's ok, Aisha.
The doctors at the
hospital will make
you feel better."

Mom and Aisha go to the **emergency room** to see a doctor.

There is a man with a cut on his head,

a girl with a tummy ache,

and a little boy who has hurt his knee.

"How did you hurt yourself?" asks Aisha.
"I fell over when I was playing basketball,"
he answers.

"Aisha Stevens!"

calls Nurse Sally. "Follow me!"

11

"Hello Aisha,
I'm Dr. Berry.
Oh dear, what
has happened?"

"I was playing Frisbee and I fell
over and hurt my arm," says Aisha.

"That sounds painful! Where does it hurt?"

"Here," says Aisha.

Dr. Berry gently **examines** her arm. It might be broken. We'll take an X-ray to be sure."

13

"What's an X-ray? Does it hurt?"

"No, it's just a special photograph of your bones."

"There's no need to be scared!" says Mom.

"Hello Aisha, I'm Dr. Michaels.
I'm going to take an X-ray
of your arm."

"Put your arm on this table so
I can move this camera over it."

15

Aisha and Mom go back to Dr. Berry's **cubicle**.
"Right then, let's have a look shall we?"

Dr. Berry turns on the light behind a big, white box on the wall, and clips Aisha's X-ray to it.

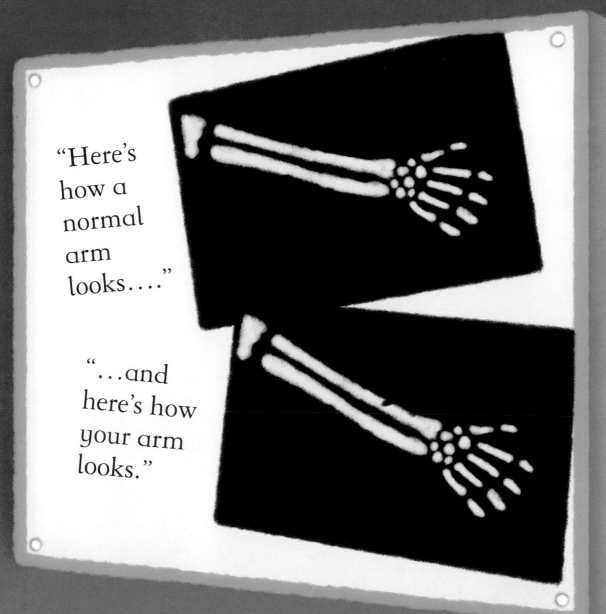

"Here's how a normal arm looks...."

"...and here's how your arm looks."

"I'll have to put a **cast** on your arm."

"What's a cast?"

"A cast holds your bones in the right position so they can **heal** properly."

"Would you like a blue, yellow, or green cast?" asks the **plaster technician**.

"A green one, please!"

19

Dr. Berry washes Aisha's arm.

The plaster technician prepares the cast.

Then she carefully put the cast on Aisha's arm.

"It might be a bit itchy, but your arm will only take a few weeks to heal."

Aisha and Mom go home.
Aisha rushes into the kitchen.

"Amir! Look at my cast!"

22

"It matches our Frisbee! Does it hurt?"

"Yes, but not as much as it did."

23

Glossary

Cast A hard bandage that is put over a broken arm or leg to protect it.

Cubicle Part of a room that is separated off, usually used by doctors to examine people.

Emergency room The part of a hospital that people go to if they are hurt in an accident or suddenly feel unwell.

Examine To look at something carefully to see what is wrong.

Heal When a part of the body repairs itself and becomes healthy again.

Plaster technician
Someone who makes a cast and puts it on broken bones.